My Very First
BIBLE

Written by Juliet David
Illustrations by Helen Prole

Published by Candle Books
an imprint of
Lion Hudson plc
Wilkinson House, Jordan Hill Road,
Oxford OX2 8DR, England
www.lionhudson.com/candle

ISBN 978 1 78128 169 7
e-ISBN 978 1 78128 194 9

First edition 2008
This edition 2015

A catalogue record for this book is available from the British Library

Printed and bound in China, October 2014, LH06

My Very First
BIBLE

Juliet David
Illustrations by Helen Prole

CANDLE
BOOKS

Contents

God's Wonderful World

In the beginning there were no people.

No animals.

No trees.

No sun.

No world at all!

Then God said, "Let there be light!"

And there was light.

"Let there be sea and sky," said God.

   "Let there be hills and rivers;

   sun, moon, and stars!

   "Let there be fish and birds,

   and all kinds of animals."

And it was all good.

What was the first thing God made?

Genesis chapters 1 and 2

God Saves Noah

One day God said to Noah,

"Build the biggest boat ever!"

So Noah and his family started building a huge boat.

They sawed and hammered,

hammered and sawed.

When at last they had finished, God said,

"Now fill the boat with two of every animal!"

And they did!

As soon as the gigantic boat was full of animals,

Noah and his family climbed aboard too.

Then it rained so hard that the whole earth flooded.

But God kept Noah, his family,

and all the animals safe in the huge boat.

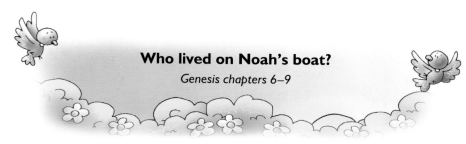

Who lived on Noah's boat?

Genesis chapters 6–9

Abraham Moves House

Abraham and his family lived
   in a far-off land called Ur.
One day God said to Abraham,
   "Leave your home here.
   I will take you to a wonderful new land."
So Abraham packed up all his things.
When he was ready, he set off with his family,
   his flocks of sheep, and his herds of camels.
Abraham journeyed for many years.
At last he and his family arrived in the land
   that God had promised for them.
There they lived for years and years
   – and their children after them.

Why did Abraham leave his home?

Genesis chapter 12

Joseph's Special Present

Do you have a brother or a sister?
Joseph had lots of brothers
    – there were eleven altogether!
But Joseph's father, Jacob, loved him
    more than all the rest.
One day Jacob gave Joseph a really beautiful coat.
This made Joseph's brothers very angry.
Why did he get all the best things?
So the cruel brothers sent Joseph far away
    to the land of Egypt.
There he had lots of adventures.
But one day, God brought Joseph and his family
    back together again.
How happy they were!

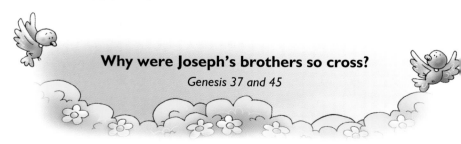

Why were Joseph's brothers so cross?

Genesis 37 and 45

God Keeps Moses Safe

The wicked king of Egypt said,
   "There are too many Israelites.
   Get rid of every Israelite baby boy!"
An Israelite mother named Jochebed
   was afraid for her baby.
So she made a basket and hid her little boy in it.
Then she took the basket to the river
   and floated it on the water.
The princess of Egypt came to the river to bathe.
She saw the baby in the basket – and loved him.
"I will look after that dear baby in my palace!"
   said the princess. "I will name him Moses."
God kept baby Moses safe.

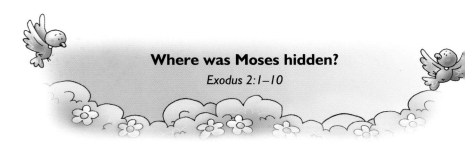

Where was Moses hidden?
Exodus 2:1–10

The Scary Giant

There lived a young shepherd boy named David.

One day he heard that a fierce giant called Goliath
was bullying his people.

"I will fight this giant Goliath," said David bravely.
"Please help me, Lord!"

When Goliath saw the little shepherd, he yelled,
"You're *much* too small and weak to beat me!"

But David chose a sling stone
and threw it at the great giant.

Down fell Goliath.

Crrrrrassshh! Thump!

God helped David beat the mighty giant.

Many years later David became king of his people.

Who helped David beat Goliath?

1 Samuel 17

The Wisest King Ever!

Many years later, King David had a son.

His name was Solomon.

One day he was crowned king too.

"What would you like to have most of all?"
    God asked Solomon.

"Please Lord, make me very wise,"
    answered Solomon.

And God gave Solomon just what he asked for.

He became the wisest king who ever lived!

The beautiful Queen of Sheba came
    from far away to visit him.

She asked him difficult questions.

But God always gave Solomon a wise answer.

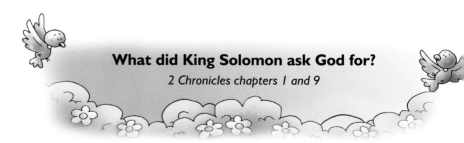

What did King Solomon ask God for?
2 Chronicles chapters 1 and 9

God Feeds His Friend

A wicked king named Ahab was chasing Elijah,
   so he ran away to the hot desert.
Elijah sat down beside a little stream.
He was very tired and very hungry.
But Elijah could find nothing to eat.
"Lord, please give me some food," he prayed.
Soon birds flew to him, carrying bread and meat.
They returned every morning and every evening.
Now God's friend Elijah always had enough to eat.
God helped Elijah when he was alone
   in the dry, hot desert.

Who was Elijah hiding from?
1 Kings 17:1–6

Daniel in the Pit of Lions

Daniel loved God.

He prayed to him every day.

One day the king ordered,

    "No more praying to God!"

But Daniel just kept on praying.

So soldiers threw Daniel into a pit full of lions.

But Daniel still kept praying!

"Dear Lord, save me from these lions!" he prayed.

And God sent an angel to shut the lions' mouths.

Daniel was not harmed one bit.

The very next morning

    the king set Daniel free.

God looked after his friend, Daniel.

Why was Daniel thrown to the lions?

Daniel chapter 6

A Huge Fish Swallows Jonah

Jonah was running away from God.

He jumped on board a boat.

All of a sudden a storm came.

The ship almost sank in the huge waves.

The sailors flung Jonah into the wild sea.

Jonah sank down, down, deep into the water.

At that moment an enormous fish swam along.

The great fish swallowed up Jonah, all in one bite!

Jonah lived inside the fish's tummy
    for three days and three nights.

At last the fish spat him out on to the seashore.

Jonah was safe on land again.

He had learned not to run away from God!

What did God send to rescue Jonah?

Jonah chapters 1–4

A Very Special Baby

One day an angel came to visit Mary.

"God is giving you a special baby," said the angel.

"You are to call him 'Jesus'."

Before the baby arrived, Mary and Joseph had to go
on a long journey, to the town of Bethlehem.

But when they arrived, they could find
nowhere to stay.

At last a kind innkeeper said,

"You can sleep in my little stable."

There, that very night, Mary's baby boy was born.

She named him Jesus.

Mary knew her baby would grow up
to become someone very special.

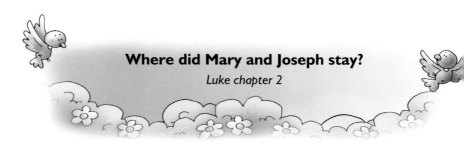

Where did Mary and Joseph stay?

Luke chapter 2

Jesus Chooses Special Friends

One day Jesus was walking beside the sea.

He saw four fishermen on the beach.

They were mending their nets.

"Follow me!" said Jesus.

   "I'm going to teach you to catch

   people instead of fish!"

All four fishermen jumped up and followed Jesus.

Two were brothers, named Peter and Andrew.

The other two were called James and John.

   They were brothers as well.

They all became Jesus' very special friends.

What did Jesus promise to teach these men?

Mark 1:14–20

Jesus Surprises a Woman

Jesus and his friends had been walking all day.

Jesus felt very tired so he sat down by a well.

His friends went off to find some food.

Just then a woman came to fetch water.

"I can give you water that will last forever,"
    Jesus told her.

The woman scratched her head.

"I don't know what you mean," she said.
    "You don't even have a water jar!"

"I have come specially from God," said Jesus.

The woman was so surprised that she forgot
    her water jar.

She ran home and told her friends
    that she had met Jesus!

What was the woman fetching?
John chapter 4

The Lost Sheep

Jesus told lots of wonderful stories.
This is one of the very best!

One night a shepherd counted his sheep.
Oh dear!
One was missing!
The kind shepherd left the rest, and went off
  into the night to search for his lost sheep.
He looked everywhere.
At last the good shepherd found his missing sheep.
He put the sheep on his shoulders
  and carried it safely home.
How happy he was that he found his lost sheep!

God is like a good shepherd.
Luke 15:1–7

Jesus Meets a Little Girl

One day a man came to Jesus.

He was very sad.

"My little girl is ill," he said.

    "Please come and help."

So Jesus followed the man home.

But before they arrived, the little girl died.

Jesus went into the house.

He took the girl's hand and said,

    "Wake up, my dear!"

The little girl sat up and looked around.

Jesus said to the girl's mum,

    "Now find your little girl something to eat!"

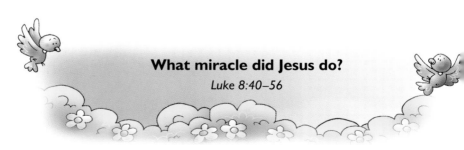

What miracle did Jesus do?

Luke 8:40–56

Jesus Feeds a Great Crowd

One day Jesus was in the country,
    telling stories to a crowd of people.
He talked all day, till the sun went down.
People grew tired and hungry
    – but there was nothing to eat.
Then a boy told Jesus,
    "I have five loaves and two fish."
So Jesus took the food and thanked God.
Jesus' friends gave out the food.
There was enough for every single person.
Afterwards Jesus' friends collected up
    twelve baskets of leftovers.
It was a miracle!

What did the little boy give to Jesus?

Luke 9:10–17

The Friend of Children

One day Jesus was sitting with his friends.
  He was feeling really tired.
Some mothers came along,
  bringing their children.
They wanted the boys and girls to meet Jesus.
"Go away!" said Jesus' friends.
  "Jesus is much too tired to be bothered
  with children today."
But Jesus heard what they were saying.
"Let the children come!" he said.
  "Only people who are like children
  will get to meet God."

What do you think Jesus said to the children?

Luke 18:15–17